2005

THE LIBRARY OF
AMERICAN
LIVES AND TIMES™

NOAH WEBSTER

and the First American Dictionary

Luisanna Fodde Melis

The Rosen Publishing Group's
PowerPlus Books™
New York

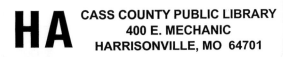

Published in 2005 by The Rosen Publishing Group, Inc.
29 East 21st Street, New York, NY 10010

First Edition

Editor's Note: All quotations have been reproduced as they appeared in the letters and diaries from which they were borrowed. No correction was made to the inconsistent spelling that was common in that time period.

Library of Congress Cataloging-in-Publication Data

Fodde Melis, Luisanna.
Noah Webster and the first American dictionary / Luisanna Fodde Melis.
    v. cm. — (The library of American lives and times)
Includes bibliographical references and index.
Contents: Webster's birth and youth — University years at Yale: Webster and the American Revolution — The creation of an American spelling book — Travelling, lecturing, and writing — Life in New Haven. religious conversion — The compendious dictionary — A greater dictionary — Old age and death — The legacy of Webster's life and work.
ISBN 1-4042-2651-6 (library binding)
1. Webster, Noah, 1758–1843—Juvenile literature. 2. Lexicographers—United States—Biography—Juvenile literature. 3. English language—United States—Lexicography—Juvenile literature. 4. Educators—United States—Biography—Juvenile literature. [1. Webster, Noah, 1758–1843. 2. Lexicographers.] I. Title. II. Series.
PE64.W5F636 2005
423'.092—dc21

                              [B] 2003010712

Manufactured in the United States of America

CONTENTS

Introduction

A lexicographer is someone who writes, gathers, or edits the entries in dictionaries. The first dictionaries were published in England in the fifteenth century as translations between English and Latin and between French and English. Modern lexicography started with the publication of Samuel Johnson's *A Dictionary of the English Language*, in 1755. Johnson's masterwork, which appeared in two volumes, presented the most precise definitions ever compiled in a book. In his dictionary, Johnson described every word through long quotations from the most important authors of English literature at the time. The quotes present readers with the different shades of meaning of a particular word. Johnson included an essay on the historical development of the language and an introduction to the rules of grammar. He included a list of words outlining a basic general vocabulary derived from the most learned

Opposite: Noah Webster's thirst for knowledge led him to study many subjects, including education, politics, religion, medicine, and, most famously, language. This portrait of Webster from around 1800 is attributed to James Sharples Sr.

speakers of eighteenth-century London and from the usage of respected writers. By publishing his dictionary, Johnson hoped to standardize the English language, according to the rules and pronunciations of the most accomplished writers of Great Britain. Johnson's dictionary was considered the standard English dictionary until 1828, when an American writer named Noah Webster published his dictionary, *An American Dictionary of the English Language*.

Today Noah Webster is best known for this publication. At the peak of his career, however, Webster was a famous public speaker. He sought, as did many leading representatives of his time, to acquire an encyclopedic knowledge of the world. He was a man with an impressive knowledge in almost every branch of learning. His public lectures on the most varied subjects were well attended. He wrote essays on language, education, dictionary writing, political reform, medicine, and citizens' rights. He was the author of the first grammar book published in America, which millions of American pupils used during nearly two centuries and which was the model for many British and European spelling books, or spellers. He was on friendly terms with Benjamin Franklin, with whom he agreed on the idea of reforming English spelling rules.

Opposite: This is the title page of Samuel Johnson's *A Dictionary of the English Language*, which was published in 1755. This was the standard English-language dictionary until the publication of Noah Webster's *An American Dictionary of the English Language* in 1828.

A

DICTIONARY

OF THE

ENGLISH LANGUAGE:

IN WHICH

The WORDS are deduced from their ORIGINALS,

Explained in their DIFFERENT MEANINGS,

AND

Authorized by the NAMES of the WRITERS
in whose Works they are found.

Abstracted from the FOLIO EDITION,

By SAMUEL JOHNSON, A.M.

To which is prefixed,

A GRAMMAR of the ENGLISH LANGUAGE.

In TWO VOLUMES.

VOL I.

LONDON,

Printed for J. KNAPTON; C. HITCH and L. HAWES; A. MILLAR;
R. and J. DODSLEY; and M. and T. LONGMAN.

M.DCCLVI.

Moreover, Webster's knowledge of constitutional matters was recognized throughout the nation. His influence was felt at the Constitutional Convention, held in Philadelphia in 1787. Although he was not a delegate, Webster was a witness to the development of the Constitution.

On the other hand, Noah Webster was also famous for his bad temper and for his violent outbursts when questioned or contradicted. He believed his opinions were always correct. To those who disagreed with him, he was insulting and mean. He was, according to his contemporaries and critics, a "vain and arrogant" man, and "a pedantic and rather choleric fellow." When his popularity reached its peak in the 1780s and 1790s, he was nicknamed the Monarch, because he considered himself superior to his colleagues. Wrote one of Webster's enemies in a letter to a friend, "I think the Monarch a literary puppy, from what little I have seen of him. He certainly does not want understanding, and yet there is a mixture of self-sufficiency, all-sufficiency, and at the same time a degree of insufficiency about him, which is (to me) intolerable."

Thanks, in part, to his unpleasant character, Webster's popularity during his life was short-lived. His ambitious literary projects left him in debt, and he was forced to travel throughout the country to deliver lectures for which he was paid. At the age of 70, he mortgaged his home to cover the expenses of publishing one of his dictionaries. When he died, he was not as rich as he had hoped to become. On the other hand, he was famous among Connecticut's most distinguished people.

Many scholars do not mention Noah Webster when writing about notable figures of eighteenth-century America. Yet his participation in the political debates of the time, and, most important, his contributions to the development of an independent American English and American culture establish his place among the most important figures of eighteenth-century America. Noah Webster was not simply a dictionary writer, but also a national linguistic educator who contributed immensely to the creation of the American identity and language.

1. Noah Webster's Birth and Youth

On October 16, 1758, Noah Webster was born in West Hartford, Connecticut. Among his ancestors were John Webster, one of the founders and a former governor of the colony of Connecticut, and William Bradford, the second governor of Plymouth Colony.

Noah Webster's parents were strict Calvinists. From written documents that have survived, it seems that Noah Webster Sr. had received a poor education with little formal schooling. He was a farmer and a church deacon, and he served as justice of the peace for the Connecticut Legislature from 1781 to 1796. He and his wife, Mercy Steele, had five children, of which Noah was the couple's fourth. The family lived in a simple, two-story wood-frame house on a 90-acre (36.4-ha) farm west of the village. It had about 1,200 residents, mostly people of British Puritan origin.

During Noah's childhood, the British colonies of New England were changing. Colonists were beginning to question and to reject British political authority. In 1765, the British parliament passed the Stamp Act,

Noah Webster spent his childhood in this house in West Hartford, Connecticut. The house has been restored and is open to visitors. There are collections of Webster's household items, such as china, and his books, including his Blue-backed Speller.

which placed a tax on all paper goods sold in the colonies, such as legal documents and newspapers. The tax was one in a long list of taxes intended to raise money to pay for Great Britain's expensive victory in the French and Indian War, which lasted from 1754 to 1763. The citizens were required to pay the tax in silver, which made paper money less desirable and less valuable. Connecticut colonists such as the elder Noah Webster were forced to barter for all of their everyday needs. Many colonists believed the tax was unfair. They had no representation in Parliament, but were subject to Parliament's laws. Angry Connecticut residents seized Governor Thomas Fitch. They demanded that Governor Fitch refuse British taxation. They threatened to burn down his home if he enforced the law.

Colonists across New England staged similar acts of revolt during the following years. The colonies soon banded together in protest, and individuals, including members of the Webster family, took part. The elder Noah Webster, a captain of the militia, organized a group of volunteers, including his three young sons, in response to reports of violence in the escalating struggle. In 1773, in protest of new taxes, revolutionaries in Boston staged the Boston Tea Party, dumping tea into Boston Harbor at the expense of merchants in Britain. As punishment,

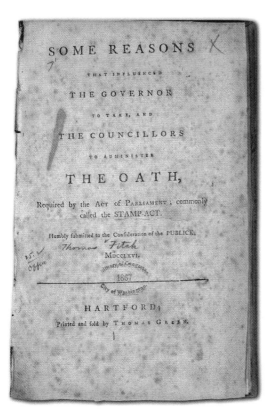

Thomas Fitch published this pamphlet anonymously in 1766. He explained why he, the governor of Connecticut, upheld the unpopular Stamp Act. Fitch's politics branded him as a loyalist to Britain and he lost in his bid for reelection in 1766.

Parliament passed a series of laws known as the Intolerable Acts the following year. One of these acts, the Port Bill, closed the port of Boston to trade. The revolutionaries held firm, however. Bostonians were provided supplies from Connecticut.

By the 1770s, the town of Hartford was more than 100 years old. Most homes, shops, and schools were on the main street. The park, the graveyard, and the church, called the meetinghouse, were in the town center. Men in Hartford worked mainly as farmers, blacksmiths, shoemakers, weavers, schoolmasters, doctors, and merchants. Women worked mainly in their homes and on their family farms. People traded with one another for the goods or services they needed.

During the years of Noah's adolescence, many changes were transforming the colonies of New

On December 16, 1773, revolutionaries disguised as Mohawk Indians dumped 342 chests of tea into the harbor. This 1784 engraving by D. Berger, made from D. Chodowiecki's drawing, depicts this act of protest.

In the 1770s, Hartford, Connecticut, was still a small town by today's standards. Most roads were unpaved. In this painting, attributed to George Frances, the Amos Bull House (*right*) can be seen. Built in 1788, the house and the dirt road seen in the foreground are typical of the Hartford of Webster's youth.

England. Such changes were reflected not only in the political life but also in the religious and social life of the colonies. These changes had a powerful influence on the development of young people, and Noah Webster was no exception.

During Noah's grandparents' time, Puritan values held sway over colonial America. Puritanism was a religious reform movement begun in the late sixteenth and early seventeenth centuries in England. The Puritans sought to purify, or to cleanse, the Church of England, which they believed was too influenced by the Roman Catholic Church. Some Puritans believed that the church leaders were corrupt. Puritans became famous for the moral and religious values that determined their way of life. Their efforts to transform the church and the nation led to civil war in England and to the founding of the American colonies as working models of the Puritan way of life.

The Puritans had seen God as a fearful and powerful being, full of anger toward all people. The Puritan values brought to the original colonies from England had urged families to devote themselves to a life of thrift, hard labor, and frugality. Idleness and extravagances were considered immoral and sinful. During Noah's early years, Puritans were still leading lives of hard work, honesty, and morality, but they were beginning to consider themselves independent, essentially good people. With time, the strict Puritan lifestyle changed. By the 1770s, colonists began to regard God not as a fearful and angry being, but as the generator of beauty and the protector of the universal good relations between people. God came to represent love and beauty. This religious revolution had an important effect on the education of children.

In early colonial America, many families had five or six children. Parents needed children to work in the house and on the farm. Young boys learned farming skills by helping men in the fields. They cleared land, built fences, butchered animals, and split wood. Little has been written on childhood in colonial America, so we do not know what young girls did in those years. We can suppose that they helped their mothers with chores in the house and maybe on the farm. In general, children were believed to be wicked. Play was seldom permitted. A child's idle spirit was broken through discipline and punishment. Children in colonial America were expected to obey their parents without questioning them.

By the time Noah Webster was born, parents had begun to look at children with more kindness and warmth. Young people were given some room for independent development, and play was allowed more freely and frequently. Many children were given more freedom, and their age, mental capacity, and temperament were taken into more consideration at each stage of their lives.

Children in colonial times were kept busy either with chores or activities that promoted discipline. Charles Willson Peale painted this watercolor of children studying in 1767, around the time Noah Webster was a young child.

In addition to a changing religious outlook, another factor influenced the development of future generations of New Englanders. The population rose steadily throughout the seventeenth century. Fathers divided their land equally among their sons. Each generation inherited a smaller parcel of land, until farms no longer could be divided into estates large enough to support a family. A son no longer could depend on inheriting a sizable portion of his father's land or purchasing inexpensive land nearby on which to start his own family. Out of necessity, the younger generations began to consider the possibility of moving away from their families. Larger numbers of young people were forced to travel far from home to look for more and better land. Others learned new skills and attempted to establish themselves in new businesses. Such was the case in Connecticut. The Websters had five children. Their small farm could not support them all. Yet, in New England in the eighteenth century, more and more young men of some intellectual ability had

In colonial times, families paid a fee for a child to attend a one-room schoolhouse, such as this school in rural Pennsylvania. This paid for teachers' salaries and for the upkeep of the schoolhouse. This made for difficult decisions in families of limited means. Sometimes children had to quit school at an early age or were not sent to school at all, even if some of their siblings received an education.

another option. They could go to college, which would prepare them for careers in medicine, law, or the clergy.

During the winter months, young Noah had the privilege of attending school, an important step on the road to independence and employment elsewhere. A colonial school was nothing more than a single, small, cold room, where pupils of different ages passed a few hours of the day under the supervision of men or women who had had little schooling themselves. Usually these men and women had little interest in children. As Noah later wrote, most of the time was "spent in idleness, in cutting tables and benches to pieces, in carrying on pin lotteries, or perhaps in some roguish tricks." The only schoolbooks available were a speller, a Bible, and sometimes a collection of psalms, which were repeatedly read and copied.

Noah's first fifteen years of life were mostly devoted to school and farm chores. However, the events unfolding around him started to arouse a feeling of uneasiness, and perhaps rebellion, in him. He informed his father that he intended to go to college. The decision to send Noah to college was a difficult one for the Websters to make. They did not have much money to spend on the education of their children. Noah's brother Abraham had decided already to move west to find a better life. The elder Noah Webster soon was convinced of the necessity of continuing Noah's education. In the fall of 1772, he found a tutor to pre-pare Noah in those subjects he had not studied at school, and, a year later, the elder Webster enrolled Noah in a grammar school in Hartford. In 1774, sixteen-year-old Noah was admitted to Yale College.

2. Education and Revolution

Founded in 1701 as the Collegiate School in Killingworth, Connecticut, Yale University is the third-oldest college in the United States. In 1716, the school was moved to New Haven, its present location, and, in 1718, it was renamed Yale College in honor of a wealthy British merchant, Elihu Yale, who had made a series of donations to the school. Yale's initial university program emphasized classical studies, such as theology, Latin, and philosophy, and it enforced the strict respect of Puritanism. However, by the time Noah Webster arrived on campus in September 1774, Yale had begun to change under the influence of revolutionary shifts in political, philosophical,

The seal of the City of New Haven includes references to the city's industries, such as showing a ship to represent the sea trade. The seal was designed in 1784 by Ezra Stiles, James Hillhouse, and Josiah Meigs.

and social thought. Many figures of American colonial history attended Yale around this time, including Oliver Wolcott Jr., the future governor of Connecticut. Noah Webster and his classmates formed a group that was considered one of the most brilliant to have graduated from the college. Webster made many close friends at Yale, and the letters he received from former classmates throughout his life are a testimony to these good relationships. Yet more important, his university years introduced young Webster to the ideas of the Enlightenment.

A Front VIEW of YALE-COLLEGE, and the COLLEGE CHAPEL, in New-Haven.

This hand-colored woodcut of Yale College, showing the chapel (*left*) and Connecticut Hall (*right*), was printed by Daniel Bowen in 1786. The chapel, built in 1761, was one of many original campus buildings to be demolished in the early 1900s. Connecticut Hall, built in 1750, still stands and is now the oldest building on campus.

Sir Francis Bacon (1561–1626) was a philosopher, writer, and statesman. His ideas about human reason became popular during the Enlightenment. Bacon's essays and poetry were probably part of the curriculum at Yale when Webster was a student there.

The Enlightenment was a period of intellectual, social, and religious exploration in Europe during the eighteenth century. The name comes from the French *siècle des lumières*, or "age of the lights." Central to the Enlightenment philosophy was the celebration of reason, described as each individual's inner light. Reason was the power by which people could understand the universe and, in doing so, improve their own condition. The goals of the rational person were knowledge, freedom, and happiness. Enlightenment thinkers taught that science and the use of reason would help society to develop. They thought that religious doctrines should always be questioned before being accepted. Their ideas helped to bring about and inspire the French Revolution and the American Revolution. During class debates and in dormitory discussions with friends, Webster learned and explored theories that proclaimed the power of human reason and the possibility of change, freedom, and happiness.

Students at Yale led a life of rigorous study and prayer year-round. At Yale, Noah learned to think critically and to view the world in a positive way. Men had the ability to improve the natural world through science and reason, Webster argued, and the best place to do this certainly was America. Faith in the critical method and a positive view of the world became the main characteristics of Webster's early work. His 1778 final dissertation, "A Short View of the Origin and Progress of the Science of Natural Philosophy," addresses natural philosophy, or physics, in this way.

Beyond the boundaries of the campus, the American Revolution began to rage. Although Webster and many of his Yale classmates were too young to enlist in the military, they formed companies of volunteers, built breastworks to defend the town of New Haven, and drilled in formation on the college green. In one of his last letters,

Noah Webster recalled that, in June 1775, the students had the opportunity to see General George Washington in New Haven on his way to take command of the Continental army, then camped near Boston. The student volunteers accompnied Washington out of town, marching to the music of Noah's flute, on which he played "Yankee Doodle."

During the following two years, the hard times created by the war were felt at Yale. Food supplies became short, college buildings fell into disrepair, and each class of students was moved to a different town in the interior of Connecticut. By summer 1777, the American Revolution reached a critical stage. The famous British general John Burgoyne decided to move south from Canada toward Albany, in the hope of cutting off any communication between New England and the other colonies. More Continental soldiers were needed, and the four men of the Webster

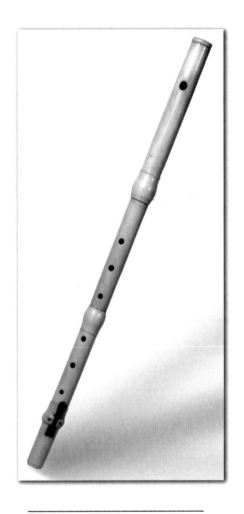

This eighteenth-century flute, made of ivory, is similar to the one Webster played as a student volunteer. During that time period, flutes were often made of ivory.

This miniature of Noah Webster was done in 1787 by
William Verstille. Miniature paintings are named for the red lead,
called minium, that was used to paint the miniatures at that time.
In the late eighteenth century, miniatures, including this one,
were often painted on ivory.

family decided to volunteer. As did many other Yale students, Noah Webster temporarily joined the regular army, but Noah's participation in the war did not last long. Only a few weeks later, General Burgoyne surrendered at Saratoga, and the Webster men left the service. The war would not end until 1783, but Noah Webster returned to school after his brief service in 1777.

Webster graduated from Yale College in September 1778. He was no longer the boy who had arrived in New Haven in 1774. His years at school and the relationships he had made there had transformed him, a poor farmer's son, into an educated man with an uncertain future. He was interested in spreading his knowledge of philosophy, politics, science, literature, and ancient languages. However, he had little interest in business or agriculture, which made him ill prepared to earn a living.

Through the fall of 1778, the American Revolution dragged on. The colonies devoted all of their resources to the war. There were few jobs for philosophers or scientists. Webster no longer belonged on the farm, yet he had no alternative but to go home. The young, jobless Webster returned to his father's farm.

3. The Creation of *The American Spelling Book*

Noah Webster returned home, but it was not long before he realized he would have to move again. Webster, an eager young man, found life on the family farm very boring. Moreover, his brothers and sisters resented his education and the money Noah had received from his father to pay for his schooling. Noah no longer belonged on the family farm, and the family could not afford to feed another child. Not long after his son's return, Noah's father handed him eight dollars and said, "Take this. You must now seek your own living. I can do no more for you." This threw Webster into a terrible state. He felt sad and rejected. He left his family home, returning only for short visits. Poor and alone, Webster decided to look for a job as a schoolteacher.

He found a job teaching school in Glastonbury, Connecticut. We do not know exactly whether Webster was a good teacher. We do know that he began teaching to earn a living, as did so many others with his background, and from there he developed a lifelong interest in teaching. Webster had already started to reflect on the role of education in society. He soon realized that Americans had neither built schools nor used them as tools for fighting ignorance. We know that he became very critical of the schools in which he worked, and he devoted most of his time to writing about education.

Still unsure about his career, Noah decided to become a lawyer, and eventually took a job as Judge Oliver Ellsworth's assistant. The money he made as a judge's assistant did not allow him to repay his father for his college expenses. He never would do so, in fact, and, in 1790, the elder Webster was forced to sell his farm.

Noah Webster returned to teaching, this time in Hartford, where he moved in the fall of 1779. However, in the spring of 1780, he grew tired of this teaching job. He went to Litchfield, Connecticut, and got a job as an assistant to the local registrar of deeds. He was invited to live in the house of a local judge, Jedidiah Strong. He started to study law again and took the law examinations in March 1781, but he was not granted a license to practice law. He took the exams again in Hartford a month later, this time successfully. However, there was little work for lawyers, so he decided to open his own school in Sharon, Connecticut. This was one of the happiest times in Webster's life. He was a member of a local literary society, and he published a literary magazine called the *Clio*. In Sharon, Noah started to study French, German, Latin, Spanish, and history in his free time. He also made many friends, both men and women. Webster liked one woman in particular, Rebecca Pardee. He soon fell deeply in love. Unfortunately, she tired of Webster, and after a short time she fell in love with another man. The rejection was perhaps too much for Webster to bear. He closed his school suddenly and left town.

When he left Sharon, Webster was again poor, homeless, and without a secure job. In these conditions, Webster moved to Goshen, where he led a very solitary life. He started to spend most of his time on the study of words and in reflection on education and school reform.

Throughout the early years of the new nation, American schools were in a terrible state. There were few school buildings, and most of them were falling down. School programs neither taught nor promoted national values, because they followed British schoolbooks. Webster's interest in education and national identity soon became his passion. He took detailed notes about school buildings, the number of pupils in each class, and the teachers. He studied the use of physical punishment as a tool to make children study. Webster proposed that children should be encouraged to study through rewards and good examples, not through physical abuse. Webster believed that America could acquire

This portrait of Judge Oliver Ellsworth (1745–1807) was painted by James Sharples around 1797. While Webster worked for him, Ellsworth served on the Continental Congress. Ellsworth went on to be instrumental in drafting the Bill of Rights for the U.S. Constitution.

> THE subscriber, desirous of promoting Education, so essential to the interest of a free people, proposes immediately to open a school at Sharon, in which young Gentlemen and Ladies may be instructed in Reading, Writing, Mathematicks, the English Language, and if desired, the Latin and Greek Languages—in Geography, Vocal Music, &c. at the moderate price of Six Dollars and two thirds per quarter per Scholar. The strictest attention will be paid to the studies, the manners and the morals of youth, by the public's very humble servant,
>
> NOAH WEBSTER, jun.
>
> P. S. If any persons are desirous of acquainting themselves with the French Language, they may be under the instruction of an accomplished master in Sharon.
> Sharon, June 1, 1781.

An ad for Webster's school appeared in the June 4, 1781 *Connecticut Courant and Weekly Intelligencer*. In the announcement of the school's opening, Webster describes himself as a headmaster who will pay "the strictest attention . . . to the studies, the manners and the morals of youth."

genuine freedom and independence only through education. As were many of his contemporaries, Webster was convinced that men were superior to women and consequently deserved to be better educated. However, he believed that young women should be taught to read and write in their native language and that they should learn the basic principles of their rights under the law to protect themselves and their property.

In 1783, Noah Webster published his first book, the product of his research on education and school reform. The small, thin book was titled *The American Spelling Book* and was called more commonly the Blue-backed Speller, for its blue cover. Webster's book would change the way Americans learned, spoke, and wrote the English language.

Webster envisioned the United States as a nation in which many people from different countries could find both a home and a job. He was one of the first writers to foresee the country's future geographical expansion and social development and to identify the consequent need for linguistic and cultural unity. In 1783, he wrote, "North America is destined to be the seat of a people more numerous, probably, than any nation now existing with the same vernacular language, unless we except some Asiatic nations." To assert America's independence, Noah Webster argued that it was time for the United States to trust its own strengths and opportunities. He thought that America should not depend on the laws and traditions of other countries, let alone copy them. He eloquently expressed this sentiment in an essay published several years after the publication of his first edition of the *Spelling Book*, in which he wrote, "Americans, unshackle your minds and act like independent beings. You have been children long enough, subject to the control and subservient interest of a haughty parent. . . . Now is the time, and this the country in which we may expect success in attempting changes to language, science,

Thomas Dilworth was an English author of schoolbooks, such as this 1770 edition of *A New Guide to the English Tongue.* Webster studied Dilworth's book as a child and later used it for inspiration when he created his *American Spelling Book.*

and government. Let us then seize the present moment and establish a national language as well as a national government."

Speaking American English was an important step for people to take in becoming active members of the political and social life of the nation, Webster argued. Webster was convinced that a national language must be taught to children and immigrants. He was one of the first to understand the importance of teaching English to people from other nations who wanted to become American citizens. Yet the English language, as it was spoken in America, had developed countless regional dialects. Webster believed it must be reformed in both its written and spoken forms. Schools must teach

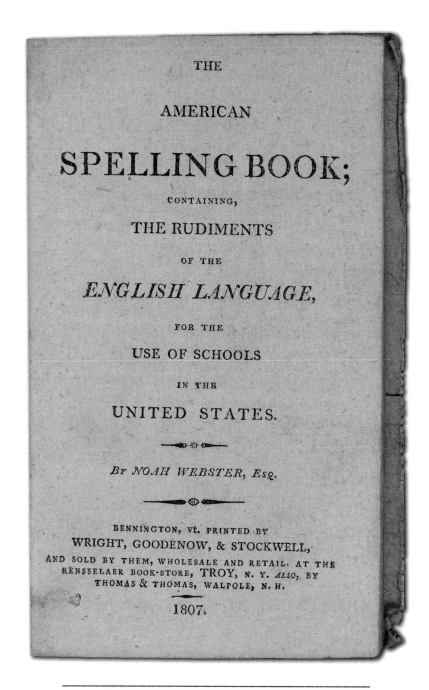

THE

AMERICAN

SPELLING BOOK;

CONTAINING,

THE RUDIMENTS

OF THE

ENGLISH LANGUAGE,

FOR THE

USE OF SCHOOLS

IN THE

UNITED STATES.

By *NOAH WEBSTER*, Esq.

BENNINGTON, Vt. PRINTED BY
WRIGHT, GOODENOW, & STOCKWELL,
AND SOLD BY THEM, WHOLESALE AND RETAIL· AT THE
RENSSELAER BOOK-STORE, TROY, N. Y. *ALSO*, BY
THOMAS & THOMAS, WALPOLE, N. H.

1807.

This is the title page of the 1807 edition of *The American Spelling Book*. In this book, Webster wanted to establish uniform spelling for American English. An estimated 100,000,000 copies of the speller have sold since its first printing.

students not only to read and write what Webster called the "federal language," but also to speak this language uniformly. To do this, Webster wanted to change "the pronunciation of our language to an easy standard;" to "reform the abuses and corruptions which, to an unhappy degree, tincture the conversation of the polite parts of the Americans;" and to "render the acquisition of the language easy both to American youth and to foreigners."

Webster hoped to improve the quality of American schoolbooks, and to give students the best instruments for studying, understanding, and using their national language. Webster's *Spelling Book* was written to reach the greatest possible number of readers. As he explained in the introduction, the speller was to be used by teachers and tutors to instruct American pupils in how to write and pronounce the language as it was spoken in the United States.

On the first page of the *Spelling Book*, Webster quoted Cicero, the great Roman statesman and scholar: "Usus est Norma Loquendi." This translates as "General custom is the rule of speaking." Webster believed the common practice of speaking a language should be the foundation of any grammar. The language described in the *Spelling Book* was based on the general rules of spoken English common in the United States, with necessary changes made to eliminate regional differences. Webster's "little system," as he called it, would give American English a uniform spelling.

From this principle, Webster developed his own pronunciation and spelling methods, which were based on a close connection between the spoken and the written forms of English. He did not think there should be a great difference between the spelling of a word and its pronunciation, as there often was in British English. Webster also believed that the spelling of each sound or group of sounds should be uniform. For example, sounds, such as the long *e* in *meat* and *sheet*, should be given a uniform spelling. Moreover, every letter in a syllable, according to Noah Webster, should be given the right amount of sound. Syllables, he added, are to be pronounced so that "the ear shall without difficulty acknowledge their number." With these rules in mind, Webster described the secondary accent, one of the fundamental principles of pronunciation that still distinguishes American English from British English. In British English, most words containing more than three syllables, such as *monastery* or *ceremony*, are pronounced with a single stress, or accented syllable, given to the first syllable, as in *MAH-nuh-stree*. In Webster's *Spelling Book*, however, these words have two stresses, in keeping with their spelling. The first stress is put on the first syllable, and a secondary stress is given to the third syllable, *MAH-nuh-STER-ee*. This adds a syllable to the word. Webster's method of careful pronunciation

Phonetics is the science of the study of speech sounds and their physical production. In phonetics, the stress, or accent, is the emphasis given to a syllable of a word. In English, this emphasis in pronunciation may be noticeable to the listener but may have no effect on the meaning of the word.

In some cases, however, stressed syllables may serve to distinguish meaning. For example, in the word "permit," the placement of the stress differentiates the noun, with a stress on the first syllable, from the verb, which has a stress on the second syllable.

contributed a certain character and distinction to American English. In describing the pronunciation of each letter or group of letters, Webster created the first training manual for teachers. With explanations such as, "The consonant c is hard like k before a, o, u, l, r, . . . such as cat, cord, cup, cloth, crop, public; but is always soft like s before e, i, y; as cellar, civil, cypress," Webster provided simple, straightforward methods of explaining the complexities of speech.

The American Spelling Book also included a section devoted to American geography. Webster listed the names of the states, counties, and cities that made up the United States in 1783, with figures for size and population. Prior to the publication of Webster's Speller, no schoolbook had made mention of the specific geography of the United States. Such information was extremely important in developing a sense of identity and place for the students of a young nation. For the first time, American schoolchildren had a reference book about their own country. Even more interesting, Webster added "A Chronological Account of Remarkable Events in America," a timeline of American history from Christopher Columbus's voyage in 1492 to the end of the American Revolution in 1783. Webster thought that the United States as a nation needed not only a common language, but also a record of a common past.

In keeping with the teacher's duty to provide moral guidance, Webster included several short stories for children. These stories offered examples of good and bad behavior and of the "American way of life." One of them, "The Story of Tommy and Harry," begins with the introduction, "There was a gentleman in America who had two sons whom he called Thomas and Harry. These boys were the darlings of their parents, who were so fond as to indulge their children in all their wishes; and even in their follies and wickedness."

The work, the first part of a three-book series entitled A Grammatical Institute of the English Language, would make Webster's name famous. It was soon known as the *Spelling Book*, even before

Noah Webster changed its name to *The American Spelling Book* for the 1787 edition. It was a great success. In the first nine months, five thousand copies were sold. Two more editions of the *Spelling Book* were printed in 1784. By 1801, the book had sold 1.5 million copies, and twenty million copies had been sold by 1829. Seventy-five million copies had been sold by 1875. In 1843, when Webster died, 404 editions had been printed. Webster's Blue-backed Speller continued to be used well into the twentieth century. Today it is considered one of the most popular books ever published in the United States.

Through a simple and clear style, "fitted to the capacity of youth," Webster wanted to provide American children with an idea of their shared experience. It was with the *Grammar* and with the *Reader*, the second and third parts of the Grammatical Institute series respectively, that this goal was realized. The *Grammar* was published in 1784. The *Reader*, which was later retitled *An American Selection of Lessons in Reading and Speaking*, first appeared in 1785. The *Reader* contained simple but elegant reading and speaking exercises for American schoolchildren. It also contained a lesson on the history and the geography of the United States.

The speaking lessons included the text of eight orations by distinguished Americans and ancient Roman statesmen. The speeches of Roman leaders, including those by Gaius Marius and Cicero about rebelling

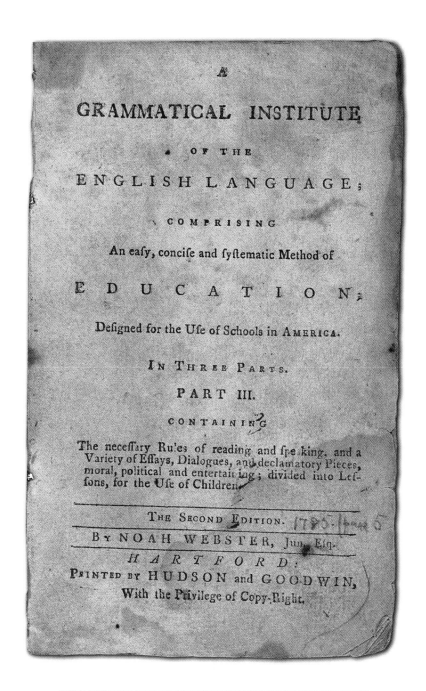

A

GRAMMATICAL INSTITUTE

OF THE

ENGLISH LANGUAGE;

COMPRISING

An eafy, concife and fyftematic Method of

EDUCATION;

Defigned for the Ufe of Schools in AMERICA.

IN THREE PARTS.

PART III.

CONTAINING

The neceffary Rules of reading and fpeaking, and a Variety of Effays, Dialogues, and declamatory Pieces, moral, political and entertaining; divided into Leffons, for the Ufe of Children.

THE SECOND EDITION.

By NOAH WEBSTER, Jun. Efq.

HARTFORD:

PRINTED BY HUDSON and GOODWIN, With the Privilege of Copy-Right.

The *Reader* was the third and final part of the Grammatical Institute. It contained mostly selections by American writers, who were chosen for the moral and democratic ideals they represented. This is the title page from the 1785 edition of the book.

against state or local authorities and fighting for a revolutionary future, are presented side by side with those by famous British and American speakers protesting injustice. The short stories have innocent, simple titles, such as "Emilius, or Domestic Happiness," "Emilia, or the Happiness of Retirement," and "Innocent Simplicity Betrayed." The lessons, composed of fifteen narratives focused on various moral themes, included a detailed history of Christopher Columbus and of the discovery and settlement of North America, a geography of the United States, including the English and Spanish provinces, and a brief history of the recent American Revolution. *An American Selection of Lessons in Reading and Speaking* ends with extracts taken from famous public gatherings which occurred in America's Revolutionary years. In the last part of this volume, Noah Webster also included well-known dialogues taken from various pieces of literature. Shakespeare's *Julius Caesar* was one of them.

Webster's goal was to spread principles of virtue and patriotism among young children. In the first years of the young republic, many people believed that America had no history or culture, especially when compared with Great Britain and other European countries. With the greatest effort, politicians, journalists, artists, and teachers worked to create a record of a common American history, a common memory, and common heroes and legends. Noah Webster was among the people who worked to create this American culture. The publication of the Grammatical Institute was an important moment in the history of American education and language. The three-volume series contributed enormously to the creation of a common heritage for the young nation. With it, Americans discovered a sense of their past and of their physical presence in the world.

4. Traveling, Lecturing, and Writing

The great success of *The American Spelling Book* did not bring Noah Webster any material fortune. In early America, writing a best-seller did not guarantee fame and wealth, as it often does today. There was no copyright law to protect the rights of authors by granting them a percentage of the profits from the sale of the book. Webster arranged a verbal agreement with the first publishers of his book, according to which Webster himself had to pay for the paper, ink, and manual labor to print his book. The contract granted Webster's publishers the exclusive right to publish any future edition. In other words, Webster assumed all the risks of the publication and gained little of the profits. Webster worked tirelessly for many years to obtain some sort of legislation that would secure authors' rights to protect their publications. As early as 1782, he traveled extensively, promoting copyright law and distributing his book to educators, politicians, and members of the clergy. It was mainly thanks to his efforts that every state passed copyright laws by 1788.

Through his participation in the copyright debates, Webster became well known among the political leaders of the time. Between 1783 and 1790, he started to take a significant part in Connecticut's political life. The end of the American Revolution in 1783 had thrown the former colonies of New England into a state of chaos. Local militias fought over state and territorial boundaries. Politicians actively resisted the authority of any centralized government, even the weak, temporary federation of states under the Articles of Confederation. Each former colony printed its own form of currency and either taxed or prohibited the purchase of goods from other states. Soldiers in the Continental army, unpaid for many months, deserted in droves, leaving the new nation undefended. The country struggled to rebuild its homes, farms, businesses, and schools, but there was no money and no centralized civil authority to do so.

This two-shilling, sixpence note from 1780 bears the seal of the colony of Connecticut. The hole in this note indicates that it has been redeemed. The lack of a centralized currency made development and trade difficult for the country.

Webster became involved in proposing solutions to the new country's problems. He wrote essays and articles about building a stronger central government and expanding Connecticut's economy. He spoke out in the state legislature concerning Connecticut's participation in the Philadelphia convention. In 1785, he published the four-part pamphlet *Sketches of American Policy*, and a series of articles on the importance of adopting a federal constitution. In *Sketches*, Webster campaigned for the unification of the states under a strong central government. Federalists, including George Washington, read and supported Webster's articles.

Some of Webster's ideas were adopted by the Federalists two years later, at the Constitutional Convention. The only major aspects of Webster's plan not included in the U.S. Constitution were the provisions for national, required public education and for the abolition of slavery.

Webster recognized the necessity for stability and order that only a central government could provide, and he used the arguments of the best Enlightenment thinkers to support his

This bust of George Washington (1732–1799), created around 1786 by Jean Antoine Houdon, is said to be the most accurate likeness of Washington. Washington, commander of the Continental army, became the first president of the United States in 1789.

case. He believed that certain liberties must be given up in order to maintain the peace and to provide services to the population as a whole. He believed that local interests should be governed by local governments, that state concerns should be handled by state governments. He also believed that all thirteen states should have the same power at the federal level in deciding national concerns. The Constitution would guarantee the citizens' rights and privileges through the election of representatives.

This was another happy period for Webster. He participated actively in the political and social life of Connecticut, made new friends, and started to travel. He travelled throughout the country to promote *The American Spelling Book*. He visited college tutors and presidents, clergymen, and statesmen, and personally presented them with the first copies of his *Spelling Book*. Webster also sought out distinguished people with whom to exchange his views on the future of the United States. Moreover, he traveled to find work and to make a living. On May 18, 1785, Noah Webster arrived in Alexandria, Virginia, where he visited an estate called Mount Vernon. With a letter of introduction from the governor of Connecticut, he introduced himself to Mount Vernon's owner, George Washington. Together Webster and Washington discussed at length the plan for a central government, the state of education in America, and the movement for the abolition of slavery, of which Webster was a strong supporter.

In Baltimore, the next stop in his journey, Noah Webster continued to meet with influential politicians and to exchange ideas with them on the political future of the new nation. There he also wrote five famous essays on the English language, originally given as lectures and later published under the title *Dissertations on the English Language*. This 1789 collection is considered by many as the linguistic equivalent of the Declaration of Independence. It is the first book totally dedicated to the study of American English. It also proposed that America needed to develop and embrace a national culture to be spread by schools and teachers. According to Noah Webster, a national government could not exist without a full program designed to construct an independent and distinctly American culture. The appendix to his *Dissertations*, titled "Essay on a Reformed Mode of Spelling," was dedicated to Benjamin Franklin, with whom Webster had discussed spelling reform after the two had met. Webster's ideas on spelling, explained in this essay, were considered revolutionary for the time. Webster wanted to omit all silent and extra letters. Such changes as *bred* for *bread*, *hed* instead of *head*, *giv* for *give*, or *ment* rather than *meant*, would "lessen the trouble of writing, and much more, of learning the language, would render the pronunciation uniform, in different parts of the country, and almost prevent the possibility of change." Secondly, he reformed the irregular spellings and sounds. For example, Webster's reformed spelling replaced *ea* with *ee* in words like *mean*, *near*, and *speak*. Webster wrote these words respectively as *meen*, *neer*, and *speek*.

Noah Webster was not interested in studying the historical reasons for why words are spelled the way they are. He had little use for etymology, or the study of the origin and development of a language through the examination of its basic parts and its earliest usage. At this early stage of his research on words and language, Webster was concerned more with a word's contemporary use than with "the sense of the primitive or elementary words," as he wrote. He was much more interested in reducing the gap between the written and the spoken language, and in providing young learners with a useful model of English usage to be adopted by American schools.

Webster's call for a national language was applauded, but his proposed spelling reforms were not taken seriously at that time. Despite criticism, Webster would publish some of his future works in the reformed spelling. Furthermore, though Webster's more revolutionary theories were rejected by mainstream educators, many of his proposed changes are very close to contemporary American trends in English. Noah Webster might admire and appreciate the language of advertising, of the Internet, of music, and of graffiti, all of which are the expression of colloquial English, both spoken and written. Consider a

Webster wrote several pieces to illustrate his reformed rules for spelling, one of which reads, "During the course of ten or twelv years, I hav been labouring to correct popular errors, and to assist my yung brethren in the road to truth and virtue; my publications for these purposes hav been numerous; much time haz been spent, which I do not regret, and much censure incurred, which my hart tells me I do not dezerv.

"At a time of life when the passions are lively and strong, when reezoning powers fearcely begin to be exercised, and the judgement iz not yet ripened by experience and observation, it iz of infinit consequence that yung persons should avail themselves of the advice of their friends. It iz tru that the maxims of old age are sometimes too rigorous to be relished by the yung. The opinions here offered to your consideration hav not the advantage of great age to giv them weight, nor do they claim the authority of long experience: But they are formed from some experience, with much reeding and reflection; and so far as a zeel for your welfare and respectability in future life merits your regard, so far this address haz a claim to your notis."

phrase such as "open all nite" which reflects Webster's principles of spelling.

The book would receive mixed reviews in Great Britain. By some it was considered one of the few books on the English language that should be recommended to young pupils. By most, however, it was harshly criticized. Some critics believed that it was not very original. Others thought the author was not an authority on the subject. Among British citizens there was a strong awareness of the development of an American speech. A "war of words" between the Americans and the British had begun. On the subject of Webster's reforms, one editorial in a British magazine read: "It is not English that he writes, Sir; it is American. His periods are accompanied by a yell, that is scarcely less dismal than the war-whoop of a Mohawk." In 1781, the term "Americanism" had been coined by Scottish-born scholar John Witherspoon. Witherspoon lived in America and had signed the Declaration of Independence. He used the term to describe a word that had not gained acceptance in Great Britain but that was popular in America. Americanisms were also scorned as "barbarisms" or "vulgarisms" by the British, and the American tendency toward change and innovation was roundly criticized.

Though the British attack on American linguistic innovations was rather strong, many British visitors to the United States were surprised by the uniformity and the purity of the language spoken in America. The

John Witherspoon (1723–1794) was a signer of the Declaration of Independence. Rembrandt Peale painted this portrait in 1794 after a portrait by Charles Willson Peale.

introduction of uniformity and purity had been Webster's major concern while writing the *Dissertations* and "Essay on a Reformed Mode of Spelling." Most British observers agreed that, despite the width of the American territory and the diversity of its population, the language spoken in the United States could be comprehended from North to South. By contrast, in Great Britain, people from neighboring counties often could hardly understand one another. The absence of dialects in the United States puzzled many British travelers.

There are many reasons for this uniformity. By the 1790s, about 90 percent of the four million residents of the United States were descendants of British colonists. Though many non–English speaking immigrants had settled in America and had brought their varied languages with them, English remained the first language of the United States. This language lost all regional peculiarities over the course of the years and acquired that surprising uniformity referred to by British travelers. Indeed, there are local variations in the English spoken throughout America, but these differences do not make comprehension impossible, as sometimes occurred in Great Britain. Especially in the eighteenth and nineteenth centuries, linguistic uniformity in the United States was remarkable.

Webster had hoped that *Dissertations on the English Language* would become a handbook for the correct use of the English language in America. This did not happen. The importance of the book for future generations did not lie only in its theories on language. It became, instead, a political manifesto about the development of American English. It was a major contribution to the identity of America.

In February 1786, Webster traveled to Philadelphia, where he met and befriended statesman, inventor, and author Benjamin Franklin. The meeting would be the start of a new friendship and a critical event in the development of Webster's views on language. The two men had many ideas in common. Years earlier, Franklin had written school primers and spelling books. Largely self-taught, Franklin was intensely interested in reforming the conditions of public education in America. In addition, he had long been interested in improving the English spelling. For the purpose of research and study, Franklin had even invented a phonetic alphabet, which is a set of symbols used in transcribing the sounds of words. The two men collaborated on revising some of the inconsistencies of spelling in British English. Franklin also introduced Webster to many of Philadelphia's political personalities.

Webster left Philadelphia in the spring of 1786 and began an extended tour of the Northeast. In New Jersey, New York, Connecticut, Rhode Island, and Massachusetts, among other states, Webster met with famous politicians and thinkers, gave lectures to eager audiences, and socialized with prominent citizens. During his New England tour, Webster earned enough money to pay his debts to the printer and part of his debt to his father, but he needed to find steady work. He decided to return to Philadelphia, where plans were underway to address the problems of the weak confederation of states and to draft a federal constitution.

Upon his return to Philadelphia in late November 1786, Webster entered the debate over the repayment of paper certificates, much like modern-day bonds, dating from the American Revolution. In the post-Revolution economic depression, many politicians had purchased the devalued bonds from debt-ridden veterans and farmers, in the hopes that the bonds would be repaid at face value. This system of risky investments was called speculation. The debate over whether and at what price to repay the bonds soon began. In a private letter, which was eventually printed in newspapers across the country, Webster argued that the government should repay the original value of the bonds to their original holders, meaning the veterans and farmers, not to the speculating politicians. This opinion made Webster many powerful enemies. His hopes of a professorship or an appointment to the forthcoming Constitutional Convention were dashed.

Instead Webster got a job as a teacher at the Episcopal Academy. Several weeks later, in March 1787, he met his future wife, twenty-one-year-old Rebecca Greenleaf.

On May 25, 1787, the delegates of the Constitutional Convention gathered in Philadelphia's Independence Hall for the first time. That day they elected George Washington as president of the convention. On the evening of May 26, Washington visited Webster's lodgings to discuss *Sketches of American Policy*. Returning to the convention hall, Washington proposed the creation of a federal constitution. The convention delegates would depend on Webster's opinions and advice throughout the proceedings. He enjoyed late-night discussions with delegates Roger Sherman, Rufus King, William Livingston, Edmund Randolph, Benjamin Franklin, and James Madison, among others. The new constitution would reflect the plan for government set forth in the *Sketches*, and, in several places, the text

---

Next spread: Webster's lecture tour took him to many cities on the eastern seaboard. They included Hartford (*blue box*), New Haven (*orange circle*), Philadelphia (*green box*), Baltimore (*red circle*), New York City (*brown box*), Albany (*yellow circle*), Schenectady (*purple box*), Newport (*green circle*), and Boston (*red square*).

Jared Bradley Flagg painted this portrait of Noah Webster's
wife, Rebecca Greenleaf Webster, around 1840.

echoed Webster's essay exactly. When the draft of the
Constitution was complete, Webster was asked to write
an essay in support of the document, which he did,
under the title "An Examination into the Leading
Principles of the Federal Constitution." The day after
its publication, twenty-nine-year-old Noah Webster
prepared to leave Philadelphia, feeling that his work
there was done.

Webster moved to New York, where he promoted his
books, continued to campaign for a national copyright
law, and became the editor of the *American Magazine*,
first published in January 1788. The magazine was

revolutionary in format and in content. Webster encouraged women to read and contribute to the publication, and he was the first magazine editor to do so. He hoped to appeal to a wide range of readers and to unite them as Americans. Webster wrote articles on a variety of subjects, including poetry, theology, law, and agriculture.

That same year, Webster founded the Philological Society of New York. The society was formed to "improve the American Tongue" by publishing the writings of distinguished Americans and by advocating a distinctly American education. The society achieved some popularity during New York's Grand Procession, an elaborate parade that took place on July 23, 1788. The parade was organized to celebrate the state's adoption of the U.S. Constitution. Some five thousand citizens paraded throughout the city in groups, divided according to their occupation. Members of the Philological Society paraded wearing the society's magnificent uniforms and holding the society's flag, which Webster had designed.

The members of the society were often scorned and their work was criticized. Webster corresponded regularly with important statesmen and thinkers, including Benjamin Franklin, but Franklin, too, was criticized for much of his work in linguistics. The recognition Webster earned through the success of his lectures, pamphlets, and political involvement had made him proud and selfish. His unpleasant personality soon became famous. He was mocked as "a literary puppy," and at times was referred to simply by the nickname the Monarch, a commentary on his own attitude of superiority and power. The year-old *American Magazine* was not making money. Not long after, the closure of his Philological Society saddened Webster. In August 1789, he visited Rebecca Greenleaf at her family's home in Boston. There her father gave Webster permission to marry Rebecca on the condition that Webster close his unsuccessful magazine and return to the more financially secure practice of law. Webster agreed.

Webster first moved to Boston, but he found little legal work there. He moved to Hartford in May 1789, leaving Rebecca behind in Boston. In October of that year, Webster returned to Boston for his wedding. After the wedding, the couple returned to Hartford, where Webster had rented a large house, and they settled into married life. Upon Webster's return to Hartford, a friend wrote, "Webster has returned and brought with him a very pretty wife. I wish him success, but I doubt in the present decay of business in our profession, whether his profits will enable him to keep up the style he sets out with. I fear he will breakfast upon *Institutes*, dine upon *Dissertations*, and go to bed supperless." In other words, Webster's limited income, dependent on lectures, published works, and other scholarly pursuits, would not be able to pay for all the luxuries he and his sophisticated wife hoped to enjoy, and his family would suffer. Fortunately, Webster was able to find considerable legal work in Hartford, and his family lived comfortably. By October 1790, Webster had been given a license to practice law. Hartford was one of the country's cultural centers, and both Webster and his wife took an active part in the town's cultural life. He became a respected community leader, spearheading plans to pave city streets with stones and to provide medical care to fight the local smallpox epidemic, among other public projects. In March 1792, he was elected to Hartford's Common Council. The births of his eight children were joyous occasions. His family was a sort of refuge for Webster, providing the strength and inspiration to write and fight for his ideas. Webster was a devoted and loving father. His children's education was one of his deepest concerns.

Webster was an idealistic public advocate. A passionate abolitionist, he was behind the creation of the Connecticut Society for the Abolition of Slavery. In 1791, Webster spoke at the organization's first yearly meeting. He believed that slavery was in opposition to the laws of humanity and Christianity. However, the cultural and political atmosphere of the southern states had made Webster question his faith in human nature. Human selfishness, Webster thought, prevailed among Americans. He appealed to slaveholders' interests by arguing that free men had more incentive to work hard. By liberating their slaves, Webster argued, slaveholders could bring about greater production and thus greater profit.

In Europe, civil and international conflicts intensified. In February 1793, war broke out between Great Britain and France. The American public was divided in its allegiance. Many remained loyal to Britain, while many others saw the increasingly violent French Revolution as part of America's own struggle for freedom. Some even called for President George Washington to step down and for French officials to seize control of the U.S. government. Rioting broke out in Philadelphia and New York City. Webster's love for and commitment to politics was strong, drawing him back to New York in October 1793. At the urging of powerful national politicians, Webster returned to journalism, establishing a pro-government, daily newspaper, the *American Minerva*, and a weekly, one-page publication, the *Herald: A Gazette for the Country*. Both publications were successful in helping to undermine the popularity of the pro-French, Antifederalist movement in America. The French threat to American unity soon came to an end, and Webster had neither the motivation nor the money to continue printing the *Minerva* and the *Herald*. Yet Webster struggled on and both publications found new stories and new readers. The *Minerva* not only survived, but also became widely read for its political, social, and public health debates.

Edmond-Charles-Edouard Genêt (1763–1834) was a French diplomat in the United States during France's revolution. He was sent by France to convince the United States to declare war on Great Britain.

Webster was a firm believer in the future of America and was a staunch nationalist. As did many thinkers of his time, Webster felt he had to do everything possible to contribute to the organization of a new world. This new world would be one in which virtue and freedom would reign. His published works reflect his views on a national political union, which he believed was necessary to acquire peace and economic stability. The basic elements of his political thinking were patriotism, national education, and political unity between the states and the central government.

However, Webster advocated these beliefs in a tone of superiority and with disdain for the general opinion, which added to his reputation as an unpleasant character and a political outsider. Many of his biographers have suggested that Webster craved the attention of a large audience to satisfy his growing ego. He boasted of his acquaintance with members of the higher circles of

American political life and declared his popularity in public. As a result, he slowly lost the influence and power he had once enjoyed. The tide of public opinion was turning against him, and the *Minerva* was on the decline.

In April 1798, worn out and largely powerless in the political debates of the day, Webster and his family, numbering three children, moved to New Haven. There Webster decided once more to withdraw from public life. He devoted himself to his family and to the pursuit of his scientific interests, particularly the study of linguistics. He abandoned his hopes for a career in journalism, and he started to concentrate again on the study of words.

5. The *Compendious* *Dictionary*

Though withdrawn from the bustle of society, Noah Webster was not inactive. New Haven was a pleasant port town of some four thousand residents. As soon as he arrived, he inspected the local school and found that it was not up to his standards. Webster immediately organized a group of citizens to establish a new school, the Union School, which opened in 1800. It had two rooms, one for boys and one for girls. In two years' time, Webster became president of the school, which then had about one hundred pupils. Among them was his oldest child, Emily.

Thanks in part to his poor finances, which compelled him to diversify his research in the hope of finding a profitable pursuit, and in part to his active, curious mind, Webster had become a scholar with many scientific interests. He devoted himself to the study of biology, statistics, and climate. In 1799, he published a dense, two-volume work entitled *A Brief History of Epidemic and Pestilential Diseases*. Webster's history became a standard text in medical school classrooms during the next century and was praised widely by scientists, but

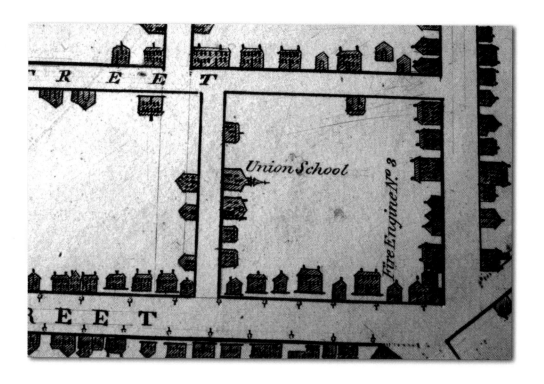

This detail of an 1824 map by Amos Doolittle shows the street layout of New Haven. Several notable buildings and businesses are identified, including Webster's Union School.

it did not prove to be a popular, financial success. Webster could only count on the funds derived from the sale of *The American Spelling Book*, which Webster spent much time revising and distributing to publishers and booksellers. He added to his educational publications four new books published between 1802 and 1812, together known as the *Elements of Useful Knowledge*.

Webster's role in national politics continued to decrease. The election of Democratic-Republican Thomas Jefferson to the presidency in 1800 dealt the

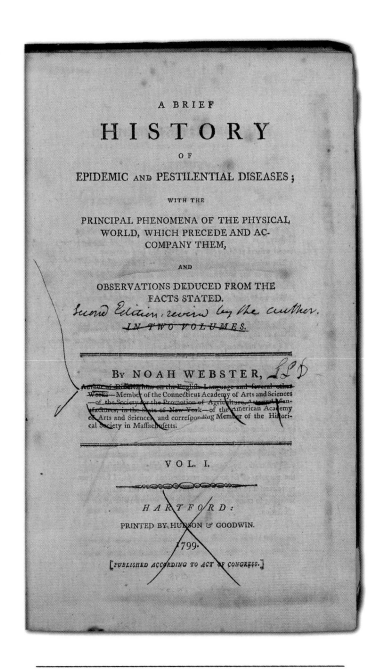

A BRIEF

HISTORY

OF

EPIDEMIC AND PESTILENTIAL DISEASES;

WITH THE

PRINCIPAL PHENOMENA OF THE PHYSICAL
WORLD, WHICH PRECEDE AND AC-
COMPANY THEM,

AND

OBSERVATIONS DEDUCED FROM THE
FACTS STATED.

Second Edition, review by the author.

~~IN TWO VOLUMES.~~

By NOAH WEBSTER, *LLD*

~~Author of Dissertations on the English Language and several other Works~~—Member of the Connecticut Academy of Arts and Sciences —of the Society for the Promotion of Agriculture, Arts and Manufactures, in the State of New-York—of the American Academy of Arts and Sciences, and corresponding Member of the Historical Society in Massachusetts.

VOL. I.

HARTFORD:

PRINTED BY HUDSON & GOODWIN.

1799.

[*PUBLISHED ACCORDING TO ACT OF CONGRESS.*]

Webster made corrections to this 1799 copy of *A Brief History of Epidemic and Pestilential Diseases* in preparation for a second edition of the book. Among the corrections he made were spelling changes that reflected the spellings he promoted in his dictionary. The printers had set the book according to the British spellings.

Federalist Party a crushing blow. Webster, one of feder-
alism's staunchest supporters, by now had lost all influence in the national political debate. However, he played
a significant role in local New Haven politics. He was
elected several times to the town council, to the school
board as school board president, and to the state legislature, where he served from 1800 to 1807. Between
1801 and 1810, he also served as justice of the peace.

Webster enjoyed the variety of his employments, but
he began to devote most of his time to one new enterprise. As early as 1800, Webster began to write a dictionary. He was beginning to develop the plan for a whole
system of education, one which would include a spelling
book, texts for each school subject from history to biology and a complete dictionary. His educational materials
would guide students through their academic careers
and into adulthood, "beginning with children and ending with men," he wrote.

In 1806, he published a 408-page book, *A
Compendious Dictionary of the English Language*,
which was a preliminary version of the greater dictionary that would appear in about twenty years' time. The
Compendious Dictionary was a revolutionary masterpiece. To earlier dictionaries or lists of words and meanings, Webster contributed more than five thousand new
words from daily usage and from areas of study including law, chemistry, and geology. Webster generally main-
tained traditional spellings. The reformed spellings he

DIC'TIONARY, n. [Fr. *dictionnaire*; It. *dizionario*; Sp. *diccionario*; from L. *dictio*, a word, or a speaking.]
A book containing the words of a language arranged in alphabetical order, with explanations of their meanings; a lexicon.
Johnson.

Webster defined the word "dictionary" in his *Compendious Dictionary of the English Language.*

Specialized dictionaries are overwhelming in their variety and their diversity. Each area of study, such as etymology, pronunciation, and usage, can have a dictionary of its own. The earliest important dictionary of etymology for the English language was Stephen Skinner's Etymologicon Linguae Anglicanae, which was published in 1671, in Latin. The author gave a classical origin for every English word, but many of these etymological explanations were eventually disproved. With the eighteenth century came the publication of a number of dictionaries that traced most English words to Celtic, the family of languages spoken by the population of western Europe in pre-Roman and Roman times. However, in truth, the origins of these words dated from much earlier. In the nineteenth century, further study produced the first truly scientific etymological dictionary, which was written by Walter William Skeat and published in 1879.

introduced, including *ake* (ache), *crum* (crumb), *fether* (feather), *honor* (honour), *iland* (island), *ile* (aisle), and *theater* (theatre), were common in America at the time. Unlike his predecessors, however, he marked the pronunciation of words by the insertion of the accent. Webster also inserted new information into the traditional supplementary tables. Webster added lists of post offices and population figures and a brief chronological history of the world.

Samuel Johnson published his *Dictionary of the English Language* in 1755. Although not the first dictionary, it was the most ambitious in its scope. After the *Dictionary*'s publication, Johnson became known as Dictionary Johnson.

Samuel Johnson, who was known by the honorific title of "doctor," had long been considered the foremost authority in dictionary writing until well into the nineteenth century. His dictionary had been created for the preservation of a fixed, unchangeable form of English, limited to the common usage of the highest social class. According to Johnson, by the middle of the seventeenth century, the English language had reached a wonderful perfection. There was no need, therefore, to change it. His definitions were made up only of quotations from the great English writers, and he believed they provided all the necessary vocabulary and shades of meaning the English-speaking world would ever need. Dr. Johnson's reputation as a brilliant lexicographer was never questioned. His contemporaries did not dare to change Johnson's definitions, spelling, or etymology. British and American lexicographers conformed to the doctor's theories on what good English ought to be, adding only a few words to Johnson's masterwork.

Webster, instead, felt that people must "keep pace with improvements in knowledge," and that a living language must not be limited, because there can be no limit to the advances of any science. Unlike Johnson, Webster was convinced that English, as it would be used and taught through dictionaries and grammars, should be based on what he called "the general practice" of a nation and on the rules of each language. The publication of the *Compendious Dictionary* gave voice to these views. Moreover, with this dictionary Webster introduced the United States to the idea of a consulting dictionary, or general reference book, particularly suitable for "students, merchants and travellers," as the title page points out. Consulting dictionaries became a useful tool in every profession.

This is Noah's handwritten manuscript for the *Compendious Dictionary*. He begins by defining the letter *A*. Webster's definition reads in part, "A is the first letter of the Alphabet."

With the notion of the consulting dictionary in mind, one year later Webster published a shorter and less expensive version of the *Compendious Dictionary*, entitled *A Dictionary of the English Language Compiled For the Use of the Common Schools in the United States*. The previous volume had proven too expensive for most individuals and small institutions to buy. In both works, Webster insisted that Americans needed a dictionary that was specific to the evolving American English.

Webster's former political foes mocked his first dictionaries and American scholars largely ignored them. Those who criticized the texts disapproved of their modernity. The five thousand additional words were branded as Americanisms or as bad language. His spellings shocked many of his contemporaries. As many scholars have since shown, however, these spellings were not Webster's inventions, but were of a style adopted in, among other texts, the court and county records of sixteenth-century England. Webster ignored his critics and proudly declared that he had made the English language purer and cleaner. His dictionaries soon became the best-selling dictionaries ever before published. However, this still amounted to only a relatively small number of copies sold, and Webster earned very little money from the enterprise. Yet Webster was absorbed in his work. The creation of a larger, distinctly American dictionary was underway.

6. Webster's Religious Conversion and Life in Amherst

By 1806, Noah Webster had begun preparing the writing of a monumental dictionary. He was also going through a period of deep religious reflection and dedication that would lead to a profound religious conversion. This conversion would have a great importance in the development of his career as a lexicographer and would become a feature of his entire written work. Webster's conversion happened unexpectedly. In 1808, his wife Rebecca and their two daughters began attending religious meetings, called revivals. Revivals were organized to increase, or revive, the population's interest in the general principles of Christianity. Hundreds and sometimes thousands of people would gather for many days at a time to hear the powerful sermons of popular ministers and to study the teachings of the Bible. They engaged in a series of intense spiritual exercises. They sang hymns, prayed in large groups, publicly confessed their sins, and renounced evil. Often these exercises were accompanied by cries of religious agony and joy.

Webster had long been against such popular, frenzied meetings and gatherings. The revivals encouraged participants to show their emotions and passions. These were things that Webster, a great champion of reason, always tried to control. The interest his wife and daughters had begun to show in this religion worried him. Yet Webster met with a Calvinist pastor. After this meeting, Webster went through a period of sleepless nights, repentance, and prayer. He decided to convert after a few months. Webster and his family still went to services at the local Calvinist church, but their

The revival movement in which the Websters participated was known as the Second Great Awakening. Revivals, as shown in this hand-colored aquatint by Jacques-Gérard Milbert, often took place outdoors. In frontier areas these meetings were known as camp meetings.

attitude toward religion had intensified. From that moment on, religion was a great escape from the sad and discouraging events of Webster's life. Religion filled his thoughts. As early as 1822, Webster began to write a new version of the Bible, which he published in 1835. He considered this work the most important of his life.

Committed to writing, Webster was forced to live in poverty. As he wrote to a friend in 1811, "My own resources are almost exhausted & in a few days I shall sell my house to get bread for my children." He decided to find refuge in Amherst, Massachusetts, a small, Federalist, Calvinist community, where the Websters could live cheaply in a small cottage. The family, including seven children, Webster, and his wife, moved to Amherst in September 1812. They would remain there until 1822. His older children, especially the young women, were not happy to live a secluded country life.

In Amherst, while continuing an extensive study of more than twenty world languages, Webster took part in local politics, was a regular visitor to the local Calvinist church, and devoted much of his time to his children, who ranged in age from toddler to teenager. Webster was also among the founders of Amherst Academy, a preparatory school that opened in 1815. In 1820, Webster was the honored speaker at the official opening of the nearby Amherst College.

In 1816, Webster signed an important contract with the original publishers of *The American Spelling Book*,

Hudson & Goodwin, who had been publishing the highly successful *Spelling Book* for more than thirty years. The 1816 contract gave the publishers the right to publish the book for the following fourteen years. In exchange for this right, Noah Webster received $23,000 in advance and the assurance that his fourteen-year-old son, William, would be employed in the firm as a young apprentice. William's apprenticeship would prove to be short-lived, and Webster would experience one tragedy after another in the coming years, including the deaths of a brother, a daughter, a son-in-law, and a grandchild. With a newfound financial security, Webster would again devote his full attention to the enormous work of writing what would be, in its day, the most complete dictionary ever published in the English language.

7. A Greater Dictionary

With his financial situation temporarily settled, Noah Webster turned his attention to the study of more than twenty languages. It is believed that, by 1821, he had mastered twenty languages, including Celtic and Teutonic, which were spoken in western and northern Europe during pre-Roman and Roman times; Sanskrit, an ancient language of India; and Anglo-Saxon, or Old English, the language of Britain between A.D. 600 and A.D. 1100. This research, he believed, was necessary before undertaking the writing of his complete dictionary. His method of study became quite popular. He laid his reference books and dictionaries of other languages on the table and worked by moving from book to book. Each word was methodically checked in each language, and he took detailed notes. This type of research meant a great amount of physical as well as intellectual work. Webster often complained of exhaustion, and as his study came to an end he suffered from intense soreness in his hand.

Noah Webster used this desk for much of his life. His son, William G. Webster, inscribed a note about his father inside the drawer, "On this table my father wrote the American Dictionary and other works during the last fifty years of his life."

After compiling the entries of the first two letters of the alphabet, Webster realized that he needed to do further studies on languages. For ten years, he set aside his work on the dictionary and compiled his *Synopsis of Words in Twenty Languages*. The *Synopsis* was never published, but a summary of the work would appear in the introduction to *An American Dictionary of the English Language*. Webster was passionate about the *Synopsis*, and he strongly believed the work would grant him a measure of immortality.

After Webster's death, scholars proved that the *Synopsis* had been conceived based on mistaken theories. Webster had ignored important contemporary discoveries of German and British linguists who had studied the common origins of world languages. Webster had rejected the idea of language as a human invention. He believed that language was a divine phenomenon that had been present since the creation of the world. Webster believed that the languages of the world evolved from Chaldee, which was an ancient Middle Eastern language that some people believed was the language spoken by biblical figures such as Noah. Moreover, Webster accepted the biblical story of the Tower of Babel as the only explanation for the differentiation of world languages. According to this story, the Babylonians wanted to make a name for themselves by building a mighty city and a tower "with its top in the heavens." God wanted to punish the Babylonians for their pride and materialism. He disrupted the work by making each laborer speak a different language. They could no longer understand one another. The city was never completed, and the people were dispersed over the earth. Today language scholars use more scientific ways to study how languages develop and spread, and Webster's biblical explanations are no longer used. However, the *Synopsis*, as it appeared in the *American Dictionary*, should be praised for its serious examination of the

In the biblical story of the Tower of Babel, the Babylonians wanted to build a tower to draw attention to their city. God disrupted their work by making the workers unable to understand one another's language. The tower was never finished, and the people of Babylon scattered over the earth. This story is sometimes seen as an attempt to explain the different languages in the world.

relationships among words from different languages and for its understanding of the influence of Anglo-Saxon on modern English.

In 1822, Webster decided to return to New Haven to complete his dictionary. His work was going well, and he was financially secure. Some 350,000 copies of *The American Spelling Book* were sold each year, the royalties from which provided a comfortable income for Webster and his family. Soon after his return to

New Haven, Webster started to consider the possibility of traveling to Europe. He urgently needed to consult additional foreign dictionaries, and he wanted to study some scientific terms in depth. He believed both could be done only in the great libraries of Europe, which were greater in number and richer in resources than were the libraries in the United States. In June 1824, with the scrawled pages of his dictionary in hand, Webster boarded a ship bound for Europe. Accompanying Webster was his son William, who would be his secretary and copier during the trip.

This 1824 painting by Augustus Earle, *Scudding Before a Heavy Westerly Gale off the Cape, lat. 44 deg.*, depicts the rough weather travelers sometimes faced at sea.

The Bibliothèque du Roi, France's first royal library, was built during the reign of King Charles V (1364–1380). As it grew, the library moved several times, eventually to the Mazarin Palace in Paris. It was renamed the Bibliothèque Nationale in 1795.

Sixty-six-year-old Noah Webster arrived in Paris and embarked on the enormous effort of consulting the volumes of the famous Bibliothèque Nationale. After six weeks of rigorous work, father and son went to England, where they settled in Cambridge. There Webster's work proceeded with much satisfaction, and, in January 1825, he wrote the last entry of the dictionary. Of that momentous event he later wrote, "When I had come to the last word, I was seized with a trembling which made it somewhat difficult to hold my pen steady for writing. The cause seems to have been the thought that I might not then live to finish the work, or the thought that I was so near the end of my labours. But I summoned strength to finish the last word, and then walking about the room a few minutes I recovered."

The following month he was in London, where he hoped to find a British publisher for his new dictionary. He was unsuccessful. Not a single publishing firm was willing to support his endeavor. He could do nothing more but pack up the pages of his dictionary once again and sail back to America. At home he found a publisher for his work. In November 1828, publisher Sherman Converse of New York published *An American Dictionary of the English Language* in two quarto volumes. Besides containing a listing of words, the dictionary also contained an "Advertisement," a preface, and two essays, "An Introductory Dissertation on the Origin, History and Connection of the Languages of Western Asia and of Europe" and "A Concise Grammar of the English Language."

Webster believed that this volume would resolve all uncertainty about spelling, definitions, and etymology left by Samuel Johnson and other lexicographers. *An American Dictionary of the English Language* included seventy thousand words, more entries than any previously published dictionary had contained. It presented not only words in daily usage but new scientific

Many scholars in the nineteenth century believed in the principle of analogy. This means that the pronunciation of one word follows that of another word, which is similar in length and structure, regardless of phonetic principles. When a child learns to speak, for example, he or she tends to regularize irregular forms by analogy with the more regular and productive structures. A child will tend to say "comed" rather than "came," dived" rather than "dove," and so on. With respect to pronunciation, a child might have difficulty with the distinct sound of "ch" in the words "chase" and "character." These mistakes are evidence that he or she is in the process of learning the rules of language. The child will go on to unlearn some of the analogical forms and adopt the anomalous, or unusual, forms in speech.

terms as well. As the title page noted, definitions were accompanied by pronunciation guides that presented "the genuine orthography and pronunciation of words, according to general usage, or to just principles of analogy" and by etymological notes that explained "the origin, similarities and primary meaning of English words."

Webster was the first scholar to create a dictionary that was encyclopedic in its scope and able to embrace the modern sciences. He presented this dictionary to a wide audience. He strove to include words that could be easily understood by businessmen and scholars, by farmers and merchants, and especially by those without much education or training. He replaced the old-fashioned definitions of earlier, specialized dictionaries. He also introduced four thousand new words from the industrial, scientific, and technical world, including *nitric, phosphorescent, planetarium, sulphate,* and *sulphuric.* The *American Dictionary* was the first to include commonly used nouns such as *iceberg, malpractice,* and *maltreatment,* and verbs such as *explode, magnetize,* and *revolutionize.* Webster also documented many Native American words, most of Algonquian origin, which had been present in spoken and written English since the seventeenth century. These included *hickory, moccasin,* and *opossum.* From French, Webster included commonly borrowed words such as *bateau, bureau,* and *prairie.* From Dutch he adopted *sleigh*, *stoop*, *scow*, and *span*. From Spanish he included *avocado*, *chili*, and *ocelot*.

Webster denied the influence of Samuel Johnson's dictionary on his own and openly criticized Johnson's style. Though many scholars have proven that Webster's definitions were influenced by the British

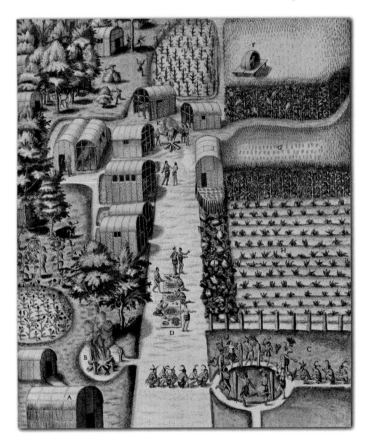

Algonquian words and words from other Native American languages were adapted into American English. Many of these were words for animals or plants that were unique to North America, which meant that there were no English words to describe them. This engraving of an Algonquin village, entitled *The Village of Secotan*, was created by Theodore de Bry in the late 16th century.

lexicographer's, Webster's and Johnson's dictionaries differ in important ways. Johnson loved elegant quotations and poetic descriptions. Webster preferred the less elegant device of long and precise definitions. Only occasionally did Webster use quotations, instead leaving the reader "to rest on the authority of the lexicographer." Who needs, he added, "extracts from three authors . . . to prove or illustrate the literal meaning of hand?" Consider both Webster's and Johnson's entry for the word *lion.* Johnson wrote: "The fiercest and most magnanimous of four-footed beasts." Webster's definition reads: "A Quadruped of the genus Felis, very strong, fierce and rapacious. The largest lions are eight or nine feet in length. The male has a thick head, beset with long bushy hair of a yellowish color. The lion is native of Africa and the warm climates of Asia. His aspect is noble, his gait stately, | and his roar tremendous." It would be hard to identify a lion or differentiate it from a bear or a wolf using Samuel Johnson's definition. Webster's definition, by contrast, is scientific and encyclopedic. When Webster did use quotations to illustrate the various meanings of a word, they differed from Johnson's. Webster's patriotism was clear. He included quotations taken only from American authors or from the Bible.

Webster proved truly inventive and modern in introducing, in both of his published dictionaries, a new American spelling and a small, peculiar American English vocabulary. Yet, by 1828, Noah Webster had almost completely abandoned his extreme theories on America's cultural independence from England. The development of cultural and linguistic differences between the two countries, he had come to believe, was to be understood as natural transformations, not as acts of revolution. Americanisms, he believed, had been coined and used because they expressed the natural geographic, historical, and social separation of the two countries. Webster's few changes in orthography were not to be regarded, as before, as attempts to build up an American language, but as a proposal to unify the language as it was spoken in both countries. The younger Webster would have chosen the title *A Dictionary of American English*. The more mature Webster named his 1828 work *An American Dictionary of the English Language.*

However, among the changes introduced by Webster, it is important to name a few that remain a part of American English today. In the 1828 dictionary, Webster dropped the final *K* in words like *public*, *logic*, and *music*. The ending *-yze* or *-ize* replaced the British *-ise* in verbs such as *analyze*, *characterize*, *methodize*, and *patronize*. Webster abandoned his earlier alternate spellings such as *lepard*, *croud*, *lettice*, and *soop*, but he continued to promote *chimist*, *porpess*, and *ax* in the 1828 dictionary. Webster's 1828 spellings of *defense*, *offense*, and *pretense*, all of which are spelled with a *C* instead of an *S* in British English, are well established in the United States today, as are *center* for *centre* and *meter* for *metre*. Similarly, Webster's uniform use of the ending *-or* to replace the British *-our* is well established in America in words such as *honor, error,* and *candor*. When adding *-ing* to a verb, he favored doubling the consonant in verbs ending in a short vowel plus a single consonant, when the last syllable is stressed, for example, in *compelling*. He did not favor doubling the consonant when any other syllable is stressed, for example, in the word *leveling*. The spellings proposed in the *American Dictionary* make clear that Webster had become more conservative in his spellings.

In pronunciation, Webster's dictionary did not prove very revolutionary. He cited only small differences in pronunciation from British English. Webster was in the vanguard of modern lexicography in his rule of the secondary stress on the second-to-last syllable in words such as *secretary, ordinary,* and *preparatory*. This rule had been introduced by Webster in his 1783 *Spelling Book* as a reading method for young pupils. Webster believed that each syllable in a word should be pronounced, and that each syllable should receive a "due portion of sounds." In British English, instead, long words keep only one main accent. The word *ordinary*, for example, has only one accent, on the first syllable.

In the United States and Europe, Webster's dictionary was praised as a great literary achievement. People saw Webster's dictionary as a patriotic, Christian masterpiece, and to criticize it was to challenge these popular beliefs. *An American Dictionary of the English Language* was also the last one-man undertaking in the history of lexicography. Webster had devoted twenty years of his life to his dictionary's creation and had earned its unique place in history.

8. Webster's Final Years

The next fifteen years of Noah Webster's life were devoted mainly to writing and to promoting his works. Between the publication of *An American Dictionary of the English Language* in 1828, and his death in 1843, he published twelve more works. In 1830, Webster went in person to convince the members of the House of Representatives to adopt a national copyright law that would improve on the copyright law of 1790. His journey to Washington, D.C., proved successful. He was invited to have dinner with President Andrew Jackson and was given a seat on the president's right-hand side, a position of honor. During this memorable visit, Webster also gave a public speech on the English language in the hall of the House of Representatives. A few days later, he was among those of the public admitted to a meeting of the House. There he witnessed the passing of the copyright bill for which he had campaigned. The law gave authors exclusive rights to their own works for twenty-eight years and rights of renewal to their widows and children for fourteen years. Webster's goal had been reached.

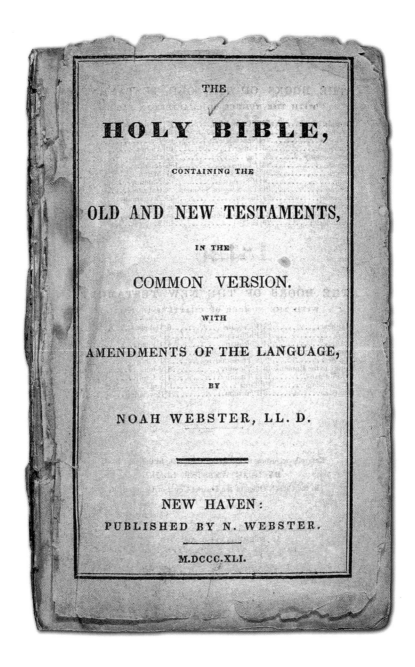

One of Webster's projects in his final years was the creation of a new version of the Bible. He hoped that the language used in it would be more understandable to all people. Webster said at the time that it was the achievement of which he was the proudest.

During the 1830s, Webster also devoted his time and attention to the many spellers and grammar books written by others that were being sold during those years. He disregarded those that had sold poorly, and he devoted much critical attention to those that had sold well. He considered one in particular to be a threat. It had been written by Lyman Cobb, and Webster attacked it harshly, both in his private papers and in public. He wrote a new version of his 1783 speller, called the *Elementary Spelling Book*, which was published in 1834. It sold successfully throughout the United States well into the twentieth century. Other important enterprises of his last years were writing *History of the United States* and his version of the Bible. Webster's revision of the Bible was aimed at eliminating expressions that he considered offensive and at improving the general comprehension of the text among readers. He once said that he considered this work the most important of his life.

His book *Observations on Language*, published in 1839, was a summary of all his life's work on language. In 1839, to his family's horror, he also announced his intention to mortgage his house to sustain the publication of the new edition of *An American Dictionary of the English Language*. With his usual energy, he pursued this goal while continuing to advertise his published works, both personally and with the help of a number of hired sales agents.

Noah Webster is buried in Grove Street Cemetery, which is near Yale University's campus in New Haven, Connecticut. Rebecca Greenleaf Webster, as well as several of the Webster children, is buried nearby.

In 1842, at the age of eighty-five, he was still very much devoted to the publication and sale of all his books, old and new. He continued to take a personal interest in contacting the various publishers and agents and in discussing his copyright privileges with them. That year the Webster family gathered to celebrate the golden wedding anniversary of Noah and Rebecca Webster. For the occasion, some thirty-five children, grandchildren, and great-grandchildren visited the elderly Websters in New Haven. As a show of thanks and religious devotion, Noah Webster gave each guest an autographed copy of his revised version of the Bible.

Early in 1843, Noah Webster finished a collection of articles he had written during the course of ten years. He continued to write until a few weeks before his death, though he stopped using angry tones. He managed to spend his last days surrounded by his family and friends. Many distinguished Americans came to pay him a visit, among them the president and members of the faculty of Yale College. In mid-May 1843, Webster grew seriously ill. On May 28, he died in the comfort of his home, surrounded by his beloved wife and children and the Reverend Moses Stuart, the pastor who had welcomed Webster into the Calvinist Church.

9. The Legacy of Webster's Life and Work

Noah Webster was not simply a schoolmaster or an educator. He was a representative of his time. His life and achievements, both literary and scientific, clearly reflect the political and cultural developments that occurred in the United States after the signing of the Declaration of Independence. As did many of his era, he possessed an incredibly vast knowledge in many scientific fields, and he was active in the political and cultural debates of his time. As were his contemporaries, he was of two worlds, that of colonial New England and that of the young United States. In other words, Noah Webster is a true representative of the early American.

In particular, our debt to Noah Webster lies in the field of language study. He was among the first scholars in his country to discuss publicly the need for the young nation to acquire a national culture and above all a national language. He was among the first scholars to recognize the differences in speech between British and American people and to put these differences into writing. His contribution to the development of lexicography

A bronze and granite memorial statue of Noah Webster was erected
in 1914 on the campus of Amherst College in Amherst, Massachusetts.
It was originally in front of Stearns Church, but was relocated in
1938 to the front of Walker Hall.

in the United States was also very important. Not only
did he add many new words of North American origin
to his dictionary, but also he introduced the United
States to the use of a consulting technical dictionary
in school and the workplace. Finally, his method of
describing and explaining words set the trend for modern dictionaries.

Noah Webster's participation in all aspects of
American life, his active and serious commitment to

everything he did, and especially his contribution to the creation of a national consciousness of language, culture, and history, must be remembered when one considers the formation and codification of America's literature, language, and history.

Timeline

1755	Samuel Johnson publishes *A Dictionary of the English Language.*
1758	Noah Webster is born in West Hartford, Connecticut, on October 16.
1774	Webster begins at Yale College.
1776	The American Revolution begins.
1778	Webster graduates from Yale College.
1779–1783	Noah Webster teaches at schools in West Hartford and Sharon, Connecticut. He studies law and teaches in Goshen, New York.
1783	The American Revolution ends. *The American Spelling Book* is published.
1784–1785	Webster publishes Part II and III of A Grammatical Institute of the English Language and *Sketches of American Policy.*
1785–86	Webster travels around the country to promote sales of his textbooks and to secure copyright legislation. He moves to Philadelphia.
1787–89	Webster moves to New York City and founds the *American Magazine.* He publishes *Dissertations on the English Language.*
1789	Webster marries Rebecca Greenleaf, and the couple moves to Hartford. On July 14, the French Revolution begins.

1793	Webster moves to New York City again and begins the publication of the journal *American Minerva*.
1798	Webster moves to New Haven, Connecticut, where he serves in the state legislature.
1806	Webster publishes *A Compendious Dictionary of the English Language*.
1812	On June 19, the War of 1812 begins.
1812–1821	Webster moves to Amherst, Massachusetts, where he serves in the state legislature and helps to found Amherst College.
1822–1830	Webster moves back to New Haven. He travels to France and England to conduct research for his dictionary. *An American Dictionary for the English Language* is published in 1828. Webster visits Washington, D.C., to sustain copyright legislation.
1831–1843	Webster publishes more school books, articles, and letters. He also creates his own version of the Bible.
1843	On May 28, Noah Webster dies.

Glossary

abolitionist (a-buh-LIH-shun-ist) A person who worked to end slavery.

accent (AK-sent) The extra force given to a syllable of a word.

American Revolution (uh-MER-uh-ken reh-vuh-LOO-shun) Battles that soldiers from the colonies fought against Britain for freedom, from 1775 to 1783.

analogy (uh-NA-luh-jee) A degree of similarity between one thing and another, which makes it possible to explain something by comparison.

apprentice (uh-PREN-tis) An individual who works without pay in order to learn a skill or a craft.

bateau (ba-TOH) A flat-bottomed boat that usually has flared sides.

Calvinist (KAL-vih-nist) A follower of the theologian John Calvin, whose teachings emphasize a strong belief in the sovereignty of God and especially the doctrine of predestination.

colloquial (kuh-LOH-kwee-ul) Conversational; using a conversational style that mimics everyday speech, particularly in writing.

compendious (kum-PEN-dee-us) Inclusive but not elaborate.

Constitutional Convention (kon-stih-TOO-shuh-nul kun-VEN-shun) The political body that met in the summer of 1787 to create the U.S. Constitution.

copyright (KAH-pee-ryt) The right, recognized by law, to be the only producer or seller of a book, play, film, or record for a fixed period of time.

custom (KUS-tum) A practice common to many people in an area or a social class.

deacon (DEE-kun) An officer of a church who helps with church duties.

dialects (DY-uh-lekts) Languages spoken only in certain areas.

dissertation (dih-ser-TAY-shun) A long essay submitted by a student, usually for a degree.

Enlightenment (en-LY-ten-ment) A movement in the eighteenth century in which traditional social, religious, and political ideas were discarded in favor of ideas based on rationalism.

etymology (eh-tih-MAH-luh-jee) The study of the origin, history, and changing meanings of words.

Federalists (FEH-duh-ruh-lists) Supporters of the adoption of the U.S. Constitution; later, the name of a political party that believed in a strong central government and favored England, not France, in matters of foreign policy.

heritage (HER-ih-tij) The cultural traditions passed from parent to child.

lexicographer (lek-sih-KAH-gruh-fer) An author or an editor of a dictionary.

linguistics (ling-GWIS-tiks) The study of differences in language.

manifesto (ma-nih-FES-toh) A document which makes public the beliefs and intentions of a group of people.

masterpiece (MAS-tur-pees) Anything done or made with wonderful skills.

militia (muh-LIH-shuh) A group of volunteer or citizen soldiers who are organized to assemble in emergencies.

mortgage (MOR-gihj) An agreement to use a piece of property as security for a loan; if the loan is not paid back, the lender gets to keep the property.

orations (oh-RAY-shunz) Speeches given in a formal and dignified manner.

orthography (orth-OG-raf-ee) The representation of language in writing, which includes alphabet and spelling.

pamphlet (PAM-flit) Unbound papers that are published either with no cover or with a paper cover.

pedantic (peh-DAN-tik) Relating to being a show-off about one's learning or education.

phonetic (fuh-NEH-tik) Representing the sounds of speech. Also, relating to the alteration of ordinary spellings of words to represent the spoken language.

quarto (KWOR-toh) The size of a book which is one-fourth of a sheet.

registrar (REH-jih-strahr) A person in charge of official records.

revival (rih-VY-vul) A period of new religious interest, or a series of evangelical meetings.

Second Great Awakening (seh-KOND GRAYT uh-WAY-kun-ing) The period of religious activity from about 1795 to 1835 in the American colonies.

span (SPAN) To cover the length of something, such as a bridge or a time period.

stability (stuh-BIH-luh-tee) The quality of something or someone not easily moved or changed.

standardization (stan-der-deh-ZAY-shun) The act of bringing into conformity.

synopsis (sih-NOP-sis) An outline which brings together many ideas.

tincture (TINK-chur) To tint or stain with color.

Additional Resources

To learn more about Noah Webster, check out these books and Web sites:

Books

McCrum, R., Cran, W., MacNeil R. *The Story of English*. New York: Penguin, 1993.

Mickelthwait, David. *Noah Webster and the American Dictionary*. Jefferson, NC: McFarland and Company, 2000.

Unger, Harlow Giles. *Noah Webster: The Life and Times of an American Patriot*. New York: John Wiley and Sons, 1998.

Web Sites

Due to the changing nature of Internet links, PowerPlus Book has developed an online list of Web sites related to the subject of this book. This site is updated regularly. Please use this link to access the list:
www.powerkidslinks.com/lalt/nwebster/

Bibliography

Bynack, V.P. "Noah Webster's linguistic thought and the idea of a national culture," *Journal of the History of Ideas*, January 1984, 99–114.

Fodde, Luisanna. *Noah Webster. National Language and Cultural History in The United States of America (1758–1743)*. Padova, Italy: CEDAM, 1994.

Friend, Joseph. *The Development of American Lexicography, 1798–1864*. Paris, France, and The Hague, The Netherlands: Mouton, 1967.

Johnson, Samuel, Jack Lynch ed. *Samuel Johnson's Dictionary: Selections from the 1755 Work that Defined the English Language*. New York: Walker and Company, 2003.

Krapp, George Phillip. *The English Language in America*. New York: Ungar Press, 1925.

Monoghan, E. Jennifer *A Common Heritage: Noah Webster's* Blue-backed Speller. North Haven, CT: Archon Books, 1983.

Read, Allen Walker. "Noah Webster as Euphemist," *Dialect Notes*, 6, 1933, 385–91.

Rollins, Richard M. *The Long Journey of Noah Webster*. Philadelphia: University of Philadelphia Press, 1980.

Simpson, David. *The Politics of American English: 1776–1850*. New York: Oxford University Press, 1986.

Index

About the Author

Luisanna Fodde Melis is professor of English at the faculty of economics, University of Cagliari, Italy, where she has been teaching since 1985. She has published books and articles about African American culture, vernacular and global English, lexicographer Noah Webster, and language policy in the United States. She is currently working on a project on cross-cultural communications in tourist publications.

Primary Sources

Cover (portrait), **page 26.** *Noah Webster*. Miniature painting, 1787,
William Verstille, Collection of the Litchfield Historical Society, Litchfield,
Connecticut. **Cover** (background), **page 72.** *Notes for Compendious
Dictionary*, 1807, New Haven Colony Historical Society. **Page 4.**
Dictionary of the English Language, 1755, Samuel Johnson, Courtesy
Independence National Historical Park. **Page 7.** *Noah Webster*, painting,
around 1800, James Sharples Sr., Library of Congress, Rare Book and
Special Collections Division. **Page 12.** *Some Reasons That Influenced The
Governor To Take, And The Councillors To Administer The Oath, Required
by the Act of Parliament; commonly called the Stamp-Act. Humbly
submitted to the Consideration of the Publick*. Pamphlet, 1766, Thomas
Fitch, Library of Congress, Rare Book and Special Collections Division.
Page 13. *Boston Tea Party*, engraving, 1784, D. Berger after D.
Chodowiecki, Library of Congress, Prints and Photograph Division. **Page
17.** *Matthias and Thomas Bordley*, painting, 1767, Charles Willson Peale,
The National Museum of American Art, Smithsonian Institution / Art
Resource, New York. **Page 21.** *Seal of the city of New Haven*. Silver and
brass, designed by Ezra Stiles, James Hillhouse, and Josiah Meigs, New
Haven Colony Historical Society. **Page 23.** *A Front View of Yale College*.
Hand-colored woodcut, 1786, Daniel Bowen, Private
Collection/Bridgeman Art Library. **Page 31.** *Judge Oliver Ellsworth*.
painting, circa 1797, James Sharples, Collection of the Supreme Court of
the United States. **Page 32.** *Newspaper advertisement for Webster's
school*. June 4, 1781 *Connecticut Courant, and Weekly Intelligencer*,
Courtesy of the Rare Books & Manuscripts Collection, New York Public
Library Astor, Lenox, and Tilden Foundations. **Page 34.** *A New Guide to
the English Tongue*. 1770, Thomas Dilworth, Library of Congress, Rare
Book and Special Collections Division. **Page 35.** *The American Spelling
Book Containing the Rudiments of the English Language*, 1807, textbook,
Noah Webster,Courtesy of the Rare Books & Manuscripts Collection,
New York Public Library Astor, Lenox, and Tilden Foundations. **Page 41.**
Grammatical institute of the English language. Part 3, the Reader, 1785,

Library of Congress, Rare Book and Special Collections Division. **Page 45.** *Connecticut currency*. two shilling six pence note, 1780, The Robert H. Gore, Jr. Numismatic Collection, Department of Special Collections, University of Notre Dame Libraries. **Page 46.** *Bust of George Washington*, circa 1786, Jean Antoine Houdon, The National Portrait Gallery, Smithsonian Institution / Art Resource, New York. **Page 52.** *John Witherspoon*. Painting, 1794, Rembrandt Peale after Charles Willson Peale, The National Portrait Gallery, Smithsonian Institution / Art Resource, New York. **Pages 56–57.** *Map* Engraved, 1785, William Faden, Library of Congress Geography and Map Division. **Page 58.** *Rebecca Greenleaf Webster*. Painting, circa 1840, Jared Bradley Flagg, From the Collections of the Henry Ford. **Page 63.** *Edmond Charles Edouard Genêt*. Oil-on-canvas painting. 1784, Adolph Ulrich Wertmuller, Albany Institute of History & Art. **Page 66. Map of New Haven**. 1824, Amos Doolittle, New Haven Colony Historical Society. **Page 67.** *A Brief History of Epidemic and Pestilential Diseases*. 1799, Courtesy of the Rare Books & Manuscripts Collection, New York Public Library Astor, Lenox, and Tilden Foundations. **Page 69.** *Compendious Dictionary of the English Language*. 1806, New Haven Colony Historical Society. **Page 70.** *Samuel Johnson*. Oil-on-canvas painting, 1775, Private Collection/Bridgeman Art Library. **Page 75.** *Camp Meeting of the Methodists*. Hand-colored aquatint, circa 1819, Jacques-Gérard Milbert, Library of Congress, Prints and Photograph Division. **Page 79.** *Webster's writing desk*. New Haven Colony Historical Society. **Page 81.** *Tower of Babel*. Oil-on-panel painting, 1563, Pieter Brueghel the Elder, © Kunsthistorisches Museum, Vienna, Austria/Bridgeman Art Library. **Page 82.** *Scudding before a heavy westerly gale off the Cape, lat.44 deg.* Watercolor-on-paper painting, 1824, Augustus Earle, © National Library of Australia, Canberra, Australia/Bridgeman Art Library. **Page 87.** *Indian Village of Secotan*. Watercolor, 1585, Theodore de Bry after John White, © Service Historique de la Marine, Vincennes, France / Bridgeman Art Library. **Page 93.** *The Holy Bible : containing the Old and New Testaments, in the common version, With amendments of the language*, 1841, Library of Congress, Rare Books and Manuscripts Division. **Page 95.** *Noah Webster's tombstone*. the Rosen Publishing Group, photo by Jeffrey Wendt. **Page 98.** *Noah Webster Memorial*. Bronze and granite, 1914, W.D. Paddock, artist. Amherst College Archives and Special Collections.

Credits

Photo Credits

Cover, p. 26 Collection of the Litchfield Historical Society, Litchfield, CT; cover (background), pp. 21, 22, 66, 69, 72, 79 New Haven Colony Historical Society; p. 4 Courtesy Independence National Historical Park; pp. 7, 12, 34, 41, 93 Library of Congress, Rare Book and Special Collections Division; pp. 11, 13, 18, 75 Library of Congress, Prints and Photograph Division; p. 14 The Connecticut Historical Society; p. 17 The National Museum of American Art, Smithsonian Institution / Art Resource, NY; pp. 23, 70 Private Collection/Bridgeman Art Library; p. 25 Dayton C. Miller Flute Collection, Music, Library of Congress; p. 31 Collection of the Supreme Court of the United States; pp. 32, 35, 67 Courtesy of the Rare Books & Manuscripts Collection, New York Public Library Astor, Lenox, and Tilden Foundations; p. 45 The Robert H. Gore, Jr. Numismatic Collection, Department of Special Collections, University of Notre Dame Libraries; pp. 46, 52 The National Portrait Gallery, Smithsonian Institution / Art Resource, NY; pp. 56-57 Library of Congress Geography and Map Division; p. 58 From the Collections of the Henry Ford; p. 63 Albany Institute of History & Art; p. 81 © Kunsthistorisches Museum, Vienna, Austria/Bridgeman Art Library; p. 82 © National Library of Australia, Canberra, Australia/Bridgeman Art Library; p. 83 © Bibliotheque Nationale, Paris, France/Bridgeman Art Library; p. 87 © Service Historique de la Marine, Vincennes, France / Bridgeman Art Library; p. 95 the Rosen Publishing Group, photo by Jeffrey Wendt; p. 98 Amherst College Archives and Special Collections.

Project Editors

Gillian Houghton, Jennifer Way

Series Design

Laura Murawski

Layout Design

Corinne L. Jacob, Ginny Chu

Photo Researcher

Jeffrey Wendt